Brynna & Mungo's
Dream Book

Brynna & Mungo's Dream Book

Judith A. Brody

Tea Road Press™
Boise, Idaho

Copyright © 2001 by Judith A. Brody

All rights reserved. Published by

PO Box 16590, Boise, Idaho 83715

No part of this publication may be reproduced or stored in a retrieval system or transmitted in any form or by any means, electronic, mechanical, photocopying, recording, or otherwise, except for brief quotations in printed reviews, without the permission of the publisher. For information regarding permission please visit the Tea Road Press™ website at www.TeaRoadPress.com.

Library of Congress Cataloging-in-Publication Data

Brody, J. A. (Judith A.), 1941–
    Brynna & Mungo's dream book / by J.A. Brody   -- 1st ed.
        p. cm.
   ISBN 0-9708666-0-7
  1. Greyhounds--California--Anecdotes. 2. Racing greyhound--California--Anecdotes. 3. Dog adoption--California--Anecdotes. 4. Brody, J. A. (Judith A.), 1941– I. Title: Brynna and Mungo's dream book. II. Title.
   SF429.G8 B79 2001
   636.753'4--dc21

                                                                                                  2001003728

Printed in the USA

First edition October 2001

Animal support groups may purchase bulk copies at special discounts by contacting Tea Road Press™. Contact may be made by visiting our website at www.TeaRoadPress.com.

10 9 8 7 6 5 4 3 2 1

The author is providing a portion of the proceeds from this book to several animal support groups which continue to provide care for those animals who, having done so much for the lives of the human community, now need assistance themselves.

Table of Contents

Acknowledgements 7

Preface 9

Introduction 11

Nesting Instinct 16

Magic Carpet Ride 18

Peel Me A Grape 20

Needlenose Heaven 22

Mungo In Clover 24

The Meeting 26

Mungo Dreaming 28

Brynna As Sphinx 30

Mungo As Landscape 32

Midnight At The Oasis 34

Hangin' With The Homies 36

Titanic Two-Step 38

Me Too—I Love You 40

Our Lady Of Perpetual
Dust Bunnies 42

Fosters A–Z (not quite) 45

A Few Words In Homage To
Our Four-Legged-Friends 55

Fabulous Facts About
Our Greyhound Friends 61

Fabulous Facts About
Our Canine Friends 62

Brynna & Mungo's Dream Book

Acknowledgements

THIS BOOK IS DEDICATED to the memory of Topaz, our cat of twenty-one years without whose quiet dignity and gentle tolerance we would never have begun fostering Greyhounds. And to Sapphire, my sweet, silly Siamese who had the heart and soul of a Cocker Spaniel.

Also I dedicate this book to my wonderful husband and daughter who always encouraged me to capture my visions in art. They also introduced me to my first Greyhound. Friends and acquaintances who encouraged me are Sherry and Mary, and the ladies of my monthly book club including Ruth, Karen, Pam, Renee, Diane, Pat, Kim, Colleen, Marilyn, Mary, Patti, Ellen, and Christine. All of whom propped me up when I was down.

I would also like to dedicate this book to all the volunteers who participate in various animal support groups, particularly those who adopt rescued Greyhounds and all of the volunteers who "recycle" abandoned pets and wildlife into new environments where they can live and prosper. These volunteers include my friend and co-worker Para-Ni who has saved many a rabbit. Bob and Wendy who bring home pound animals when their time at the pound has run out, and who then do not stop until a home is found for the animal. Georgia who uses her home to bring in animals in need. Peaches, who on more than one occasion, climbed onto the fourth floor ledge to rescue a bird trapped in the building's shutters. And to all of you who believe in the lives of the creatures with whom we share this earth.

I also acknowledge my fearless leaders, Joy and Tom and Karen who are devoted to the love of animals. They have taught me much about Greyhounds. Lastly, this book is dedicated to all of you who share your life with a loving animal.

And last but not least, I wish to dedicate this book to my hard working and dedicated publisher, Rhonda Winchell Sharp of Tea Road Press™, who believed!

Preface

I AM OWNED, BODY AND SOUL, by two "rescued" Greyhounds. In the case of my two dogs, the Greyhound organization—one of many dedicated to the humane treatment of dogs—saved Brynna and Mungo from being destroyed after their racing careers had ended. As is the case with so many dog owners, Brynna and Mungo also saved me. They provide me with love, companionship, a source of great beauty which delights my eyes, and endless drawings and stories to entertain myself, family and friends.

As our involvement with Greyhounds has continued, we now provide temporary care to the occasional Greyhound rescued, and needing a temporary home in the search for a permanent home. Whether your dog is a Greyhound, or another breed, the bridge of love between our dogs and ourselves is universal and joyous. This book is intended as a tribute to all the dogs we love and who ask only that we give them back a small amount of all the gifts they bring to our lives.

Brynna & Mungo's Dream Book

Introduction

BRYNNA WAS OUR INTRODUCTION to Greyhounds, the breed of dog which would soon take over our lives and our home. We met Brynna after my daughter submitted an adoption application to a Greyhound adoption organization. She had seen a television documentary which focused on the harsh treatment of these animals during their racing lives and was deeply moved by it. Unknown to many is that when the dog's racing life is over, they are often abandoned or destroyed.

Soon two placement representatives came by our house with three Greyhounds in order to consider us as possibilities for adopting the dogs. These beautiful animals were calm and picturesque, lounging around the living room and feeling at home on the sofa. As an artist, I had previously worked with models at local studios or painted pictures of scenery on location, The dogs stillness reminded me of the models posing and my cooperation in adopting was cemented when one of the visiting dogs gave me a Greyhound kiss as I petted it.

So it began. One blistering hot day my daughter and her dad drove to the far side of San Diego to participate in the required course in caring for Greyhounds. This course is laughingly referred to as Greyhound 101. They were also to pick out a dog from the four "cat safe" dogs which were kenneled at the adoption organization in San Diego. They took along Ragnell, our Cocker Spaniel, a bundle of hyperactivity my husband had found the previous year when he'd been out jogging. Ragnell, whose owners never claimed her, became a member of our family. She lived outdoors most of the time, spending her days in a territorial standoff with our cat—an eighteen-year member of the family. I had taken Ragnell to obedience school, but was asked to leave when her disruptive behavior broke up the class repeatedly. How was she going to live with a Greyhound when she couldn't get along with most other dogs? Well, the answer—as we were to find out—was just fine. Ragnell went along for the long car ride, and the selection of our Greyhound, since she would have an intimate relationship with any other dog joining our family.

Arriving, my daughter and husband participated in Greyhound 101 and were introduced to the four dogs considered cat and small animal safe. Brynna (kennel name "Sprout" because she was underweight and shopworn) was the dog which came willingly when called, the most anxious to please and the one Ragnell seemed most likely to tolerate. Poor Brynna, with only a stump for a tail, badly scarred, and missing a toe on her right, rear foot (probably all track accidents) was already over five years old. She probably ran very fast and won or placed well in a respectable number of races as five years is the maximum age for a racing Greyhound.

Brynna had already been sent to a home, but bounced back when they were either unable or unwilling to keep her. We never found out why. But we did find out that her previous history had left her noticeably emotionally scarred. We soon became experts at all the types and depths of Brynna's fears. She whined when the members of our family split-up into separate rooms, much preferring situations where she could see us all together. She was terrified of loud noises. Her fear of falling on smooth floors left her occasionally paralyzed with fear.

Sometimes she would stand in doorways and tremble with anxiety over crossing the threshold. Gradually, we helped her to overcome all these fears and have never regretted one single minute of the effort. So traumatized was our Brynna that it took about six months before she trusted us completely. It also took three months before she wagged her tail. We accepted it thinking that there was nerve damage to the stump. What a momentous occasion it was when we saw that stump hesitantly twitch for the first time! It should be noted that this is somewhat unusual. Most of the dogs adjust much more quickly.

It was during this time that I began sketching and drawing Brynna. With her quiet disposition and clean, beautiful lines it was only logical to use her as a model. When I began to turn the drawings into paintings after we'd also adopted Mungo*, the stories in the pages that follow, would creep into my mind, one little detail at a time. I hope you enjoy the illustrations and that your imagination is sufficiently tickled by the stories, to stir your own creative juices into embellishing them with additional ideas and insights gleaned from the paintings.

*Mungo, who came to us named "Cagney" was a foster dog I just couldn't bear to part with. For his story, please see the section on Fosters A–Z.

Judith A. Brody

Nesting Instinct

Like an eagle in its eyrie, Mungo seems to have a strong sense of his own space. He likes to arrange his pillows until they are just right (and he does want all of the pillows!), gather his toys, and lie in their midst like a mother bird guarding her eggs. Then he looks around one last time to make sure all is in order, gives a loud sigh, and rests his head for a nap.

*Probably because he lived in a small crate where he could control the nearby surrounding area, Mungo developed what we refer to as his Nesting Instinct. He always creates a little room-within-a-room for himself when he is ready to rest.

Nesting Instinct

Magic Carpet Ride

I'm sure that all the dogs arriving at our house think that somehow they've finally reached escape velocity which has propelled them into a much different world than they have been used to. (That is all except for Mungo who appears not to have ever figured out which planet his magic carpet landed on.) Although disoriented at first, the fosters adapt quickly to the soft rugs and pillows, the good food and treats, the privilege of being able to race around the garden if inclined to or not race, if so inclined.

I also suspect that our "rescues" are getting word back, perhaps through a sort of "secret Greyhound telegraph" to some dogs still earthbound at track kennels, telling them what is in store for those who make it out. With few exceptions, the fosters come in our front door and head straight for the master bedroom where they jump onto my bed. Once there, they gaze back at us as if this is only what they've been expecting all along. (This may be why they are known as Gazehounds.)

*Magic Carpet Ride was finished just as our household dynamics changed. Topaz, our almost twenty-one-year-old cat, said goodbye to this world yesterday. She will be greatly missed by everyone except Ragnell, who can now be an inside dog if she wishes. The new foster, who will be dropped off this weekend, no longer must be a "cat safe" dog.

Magic Carpet Ride

Peel Me A Grape

Brynna is becoming used to having people wait on her. Life, at times, seems to be one big party for our girl, posing here as Bacchus. She even receives little treats when she is resting on the sofa. These are carried and fed to her, like offerings to the gods. Here, she disdainfully ignores the proffered food, while a Satyr, tries to entertain her. She has drunk and fed. The moon is full. Diana is running with her hounds, but Brynna declined. Why leave such comfort? (Are those dust bunnies under the sofa?)

Brynna is a picky eater and sometimes has to be coaxed. Often the sofa is just too cozy to leave for something as mundane as food, though she will take most anything from our hands while reclining there. I often wonder if she is saying to me, "Peel Me A Grape."

Judith A. Brody

Peel Me A Grape

Needlenose Heaven

Brynna *is dreaming.* She's dreaming of a world where cats worship dogs and rabbits chase themselves, saving Greyhounds the trouble. In her dreams every dog has a fully belly and a soft sofa to sleep on. There is always a full moon in Brynna's dreams, and she can howl and run with the pack or ignore them depending on her mood at the moment.

*Brynna is definitely living in Needlenose Heaven now. One of the first things she did when she arrived at our house was to put her front paw on the sofa and look fearfully over her shoulder for approval. Naturally she is allowed to sleep on the sofa, who could resist her?

Judith A. Brody

Needlenose Heaven

Mungo In Clover

Mungo accepts the "good life" as though he was to the manor born. He probably raced hard and placed well all his life. When we got him he was past the five year mark for dogs (mandatory retirement for racing Greyhounds). Mungo seems to enjoy his retirement—the soft bedding, the treats from the table, the continuous supply of affection, being able to go in or outdoors as he desires. He always sleeps well, and frequently, and always with a contented look on his beautiful face. Mungo likes to stretch out on the floor in warm weather. In winter Mungo likes to cuddle up with his pillows. When it is cool, he curls up so small that he looks like he's trying to fit on the head of a pin, in spite of the fact that he is eighty-five pounds of lean dog.

*Mungo In Clover is a far different Mungo from the race track edition. He must have lived in a crate for five years while he raced. As a result all the hair has rubbed off his hind quarters and the hair follicles were so destroyed his hair will never grow back in these places. Other that that, he is not badly scarred. Mungo is affectionate, sweet and gentle. He accepts our love and favors calmly and is never effusively grateful.

Mungo In Clover

The Meeting

Brynna *is greeting a rabbit* by bowing to it. Because she is "small animal" safe, she isn't making the connection between this small animal and the mechanical rabbit she used to chase at the track when she raced. Brynna is interested in all creatures, but never hostile to any. She is curious, but very gentle.

*The Meeting is inspired by Brynna's beautiful manners. She is especially gentle with my twenty-year-old cat whom she once assisted over to the water dish when the cat, napping, fell off the VCR and appeared confused and disoriented.

The Meeting

Mungo Dreaming

This is Mungo. He is sleeping. (Greyhounds sleep and dream a lot!) He's dreaming about rabbits. In his dream Mungo's wondering why he's surrounded by rabbits and why these rabbits don't look or sound like the mechanical one at the racetrack. Mungo may be also wondering why he seems to be metamorphosing into a rabbit himself. Many things confuse Mungo.

**Mungo Dreaming took me six months and two false starts to solidify the idea in my head. I kept trying to catch it on paper, and even with many false starts, refused to abandon it. The idea was just too compelling.*

Mungo Dreaming

Brynna As Sphinx

*J*ust like the Sphinx in Egypt, Brynna is a riddle wrapped in an enigma. Here she is living in Egypt when people still knew the answer to that riddle, before it was lost to the sands of time. And just like the Sphinx, this pose is one most Greyhounds assume often because of their unusual anatomy. They are built for running, not for sitting.

Brynna has been a voyage of discovery. New layers of her personality constantly revealing themselves like the layers of an onion peeling away. Incredibly shy and fearful when she came to us, we watched her blossom in our care. However, every once in a while something will trigger one of her old insecurities and we will have to reassure her for a brief time until she regains her hard won confidence.

Brynna As Sphinx reflects our curiosity about her background. Like all adopted Greyhounds, we know little about her life before she came to us. From examining her I can tell that she was injured many times, and I suspect she may also have been abused on occasion. I don't think she will ever be one hundred percent complacent and secure, like my other pets, as much as I try to compensate for her early history by giving her a good life now.

Brynna As Sphinx

Mungo As Landscape

Like rolling foothills or low mountains when viewed from an airplane, Mungo becomes part of the terrain on a bed of flowers or a patterned carpet. And like those same landmarks, he doesn't move much, except to wag his tail, when approached. Mungo is large, even for a Greyhound. He isn't a dominant male and often, in spite of his great size, he acts like a puppy. Here he is sleeping on his rather broad (for a Greyhound) back. He will also be delighted to roll into this position if he senses the possibility of a belly rub.

*Mungo As Landscape portrays Mungo, with his gentle loving nature, great eye contact, and innate ability to sense what you want or need of him. He has embarked on a second career. He is licensed as a Therapy Animal and visits nursing homes, hospitals, shelters for battered children and adults, and schools for "special needs" children, the "Special Olympics," and he's even visited Ronald McDonald House. This makes two extremely successful careers for our boy as he ran the full five years maximum that Greyhounds are allowed, as long as they continue to win.

Mungo As Landscape

Midnight At The Oasis

Brynna has a delicate, fine-boned look, really classic lines, a beauty of a dog. In this painting she is living her life as a harem girl in the ancient and exotic east. We see her residing in a Seraglio and looking through a window from which she can see the camel caravans traveling the Old Silk Road through the vast deserts of the middle and far east. Perhaps this takes place in the time of Marco Polo.

*Midnight At The Oasis was originally titled "Brynna As Odalisque" because with her delicate beauty, Brynna made me think of those paintings which are so named. However, as I was working on this piece the radio kept playing the song "Midnight At The Oasis" and the camels began mysteriously creeping into the drawing, until I had no choice but to rename it and put the original title on the back burner awaiting a future work. The two people you see on the back of one camel are my daughter and me—a totally unrelated adventure.

Midnight At The Oasis

Hangin' With The Homies

Greyhounds are social animals and like to be with others of their own kind. They love luxury and locate comfortable spots like beds quickly. If there are enough Greyhounds in one small house, even though their coats are short, dust bunnies will begin to form. This group is doing the Greyhound equivalent of standing on the corner, watching and talking. Perhaps these particular dogs are discussing Brynna's lack of a tail and suggesting places to look for it. Possibly the dust bunnies have already checked under the bed and found only more dust bunnies and are trying to tell the dogs on the bed that Brynna's tail must be somewhere else. Maybe one dog is saying to the next, "My mother said that heaven is a place with a comfortable bed for lounging and the rabbits come to you." It's possible that another observes, "When I was young I was taught to chase a mechanical rabbit. Unfortunately my trainers didn't teach me what to do once I caught one." Would you have guessed that the smallest dog in this group is the "Leader of the Pack?" And, would you have guessed that the next smallest is her trusted Lieutenant?

Hangin' With The Homies is the group portrait of some of the two dozen dogs we fostered. They often like to hang out in the bedroom together. Some of the really shy ones find a quiet corner in the bedroom and stay there for days emerging only to eat or "take care of business." Ragnell, the Cocker Spaniel, can't quite make it onto the bed. She relaxes on the floor in this picture, confident in the knowledge that she can (and has on occasion) dominate the fosters. She is not as social as the Greyhounds and normally finds herself a more solitary spot. Oddly, she gets along only with Greyhounds and will not tolerate other breeds of dogs.

Hangin' With The Homies

Titanic Two-Step

Brynna has a terrible fear of falling. And why should she risk falling on a slick surface when she has willing slaves who will ferry her across the treacherous wastes? We all pay homage to Brynna because she has the look of royalty about her.

Brynna has done the Titanic Two-Step on our kitchen floor many times. She finds linoleum a difficult place to gain a pawhold with her hare-like feet and has fallen many times. Now she usually waits for her "escort" to guide her. On occasion, she must be carried.

Titanic Two-Step

Me Too—I Love You

I*f you want to find true love,* the answer is unbelievably simple. Adopt a Greyhound. This picture needs no other explanation than the familiar saying, "A picture is worth a thousand words."

Me Too—I Love You is a portrait of Nightingale an unforgettable foster. Even though we were thrilled to pass her on, I can't resist a smile when I think of her. Her memory still warms me. Loving was her specialty. She was a really huge (even had she been a male) female with a happy, confident, good-natured personality. She needed to be someone's only dog because she liked a lot of attention and affection. And, she was not shy about displaying affection either. She was always in your face—ready to cuddle and kiss. When a young man came to see her, a potential adopter, she seemed to know that he was hers. She licked every inch of his exposed skin. When he returned for the actual adoption procedure, she was thrilled to see him again, and repeated the process. I'm sure they are very happy together and wherever they are—I'm sure he's very, very clean.

Judith A. Brody

Me Too – I Love You

Our Lady Of Perpetual Dust Bunnies

***L**innet has a classic beauty* like a Roman or Greek statue, or a painting by Rafael. She has large brown eyes which always seem to be searching for answers to unspoken questions. These eyes are set into a beautifully ascetic, chiseled countenance. She has a classic delicacy about her appearance and about the way she carries herself. She never has bad breath or doggy odor. Shy, but sensitive she sniffs out small injuries or other problems in members of her pack and appears to empathize with the bearer of such injuries. If she had lived during the time of the artist Raphael, she surely would have been the subject of many of his paintings. Unlike our other dogs which are various types of brindle, Linnet is a beautiful blonde. And whether or not that is the cause—she sheds fur constantly and copiously. She is a Dust Bunny Factory.

*Linnet, who is portrayed in Our Lady Of Perpetual Dust Bunnies, was previously a foster and came to us as "Yin" from the Y Group of rescues. A honey blonde with big, brown appealing eyes, she was shy and remains so. She rarely exits the bedroom except to take care of "necessaries." Naturally, this did not set well with any potential adopters. The first person she bonded to was my husband and it appears that "gentlemen" really do prefer "blondes" because he fell in love with her. She presides over the master bedroom which she rarely leaves and we occasionally contemplate putting a zipper in her so she can store our pajamas during the day. When guests come over, she doesn't emerge from the bedroom at all. Thus, very few people even realize that she exists.

Judith A. Brody

Our Lady Of Perpetual Dust Bunnies

Brynna & Mungo's Dream Book

Fosters—A to Z *(not quite)*

A Very Brief Summary of Greyhounds We Have Loved

FOLLOWING IS A LIST OF GREYHOUNDS we have fostered in our home since we became involved with these wonderful animals. Each group of greyhounds being rescued is assigned an alphabet letter, and all dogs within that group receive names beginning with that letter. We, naturally, did not foster a dog from each of the groups as they are brought in according to the rescue schedule, and not necessarily when we have the space for a new foster greyhound.

Aaron (Foster Dog #1) • As our first foster dog, Aaron, was a happy experience which encouraged us to continue fostering. Although a large, black male, with a flash of white on his chest, approximately three years old, he was quiet and well behaved. Aaron, though, was frightened of our cat and whenever she came near, he would take off in the opposite direction.

Aaron was very affectionate and liked to walk up to people and "kiss" them. He seemed especially to like children. He was also very timid. The first day my daughter and I walked him with Brynna, we passed a yard where a Rottweiler charged the fence, snarling and barking. Aaron was so petrified, he froze to the ground and we were unable to move him along until we each took one end of him and partly lifted him . . . no mean feat! Brynna dominated him completely and I believe she thought we had gotten him exclusively for her. She dug a "den" in the garden and had him sit part-way in it with her while they appeared to survey her little queendom. She seemed to go into mourning for several days when he moved on to his permanent home.

He was our first foster and I might have had more trouble giving him up, except that the people who came to adopt him had a young son and it was not difficult to see that the boy and the dog adored each other at very first sight. They couldn't have been separated, once they first met. We have seen them at a Greyhound event and the love affair is still in full flower.

Cagney aka Mungo (Foster Dog #2) • Good-natured and goofy, Mungo is a male who is a dark brindle in color. Originally very cat curious, he stalked our ancient cat until she was up against a wall, then gave her a thorough bath. Actually he seemed to evaluate almost everything this way. Small objects, he would pick up in his mouth as if to feel and taste them, then replace them, absolutely unharmed, near where they originally sat, something he continues to do to this day. We have a persimmon tree which had a low growing fruit this past fall. He would go out and check to see if the fruit was ripe each day by taking it into his mouth, then backing off. He never damaged the fruit.

While he was still a foster, I knew I was in trouble when I heard myself describe him to the placement assistant as "very quiet and laid back; extremely gentle, never, never bumping anyone; cooperative, making good eye contact; would probably do well in a home with a mature person or someone with a handicap—someone like me." We did keep him and my husband renamed him "Mungo" after the Patron Saint of Glasgow, because he is "Mungo the Good." We have never regretted it, even though two large dogs in addition to the rest of our menagerie has been a bit of a stretch at times. He always defers to our first Greyhound, Brynna. When someone comes to the door, he runs and gets her because he knows that she gets to be first dog in the receiving line greeting new arrivals.

Galahad (Foster #3) • An exceptionally beautiful tiger-striped, tiger colored, male, Galahad, was particularly quiet and docile. A little slow to housebreak; he lifted his leg in the house four times before he understood that it just wasn't done. An inquisitive dog who sniffed everything thoroughly—an action which involved puffing up and expelling air from his cheeks and making a noise like a distant steam engine, Galahad moved on without my chance for a goodbye. The placement assistant picked him up for adoption to a home down the coast one day when I wasn't there, leaving me with an empty feeling. I still search for him at every Greyhound event we attend.

Ivan (Foster #4) • We called him "Ivan the Terrified" because he was an unusually shy male. Brindle, like most of our fosters but with wider bands, he looked like he was wearing striped pajamas. When he first arrived he hid in a far corner of my bedroom and didn't emerge the entire day. When he finally came out he walked into the kitchen where someone dropped a pot frightening him so much that we heard an unearthly scraping noise as he squeezed his large body through a door just large enough to allow our cat to enter and leave my studio. To this day, we've never figured out how he did it without injuring himself.

He became one of our most affectionate fosters and got along beautifully with our dogs, especially the Cocker who he allowed to completely dominate him. His tail had been broken near the far end at some point in his life and healed in such a way that it had an adorable little twist at the end. This tail thumped up and down against the floor whenever one of us entered the room he was lying in. He was a "woolly" or "fuzzy," a Colorado dog with a larger head than most Greyhounds and a longer, thicker coat. Ivan came back for a visit when his adoptive family had to travel out of state and didn't want to kennel him as he never completely got over his shyness.

Jammer (Foster #5) • Irrepressible Jammer was white with tan spots. More forward and active than most of our fosters, we didn't have him very long. Our dogs didn't really bond with him as they did Ivan whose absence when he was adopted, they appeared to mourn. He liked to sleep on his back in the middle of the sofa which didn't endear him to Brynna at all. She considers the sofa all hers. He also shed more than the other dogs, or perhaps it was just more visible because he was lighter.

∽ ∽ ∽

Kahlua (Foster #6) • This was a terribly frightened, shy female passed to us after she did poorly in her first foster home. Almost the feel safest and happiest when she was being walked in tandem with our Mungo.

After she finally warmed to us, the couple who wanted to adopt her came over several times and worked with us and her so the leave-taking wouldn't be too terrible a trauma for her. They've done exceptionally well with her and remained friends with us so we get to see her occasionally. Kahlua, renamed Bijou, is so confident now, that she can even attend "Show and Tells."*

*These are events held at various locations where we set up a booth with our Greyhounds to recruit new homes, foster homes and funding.

∽ ∽ ∽

Monet (Foster #8) • A puppyish and incredible affectionate small red brindle male, Monet and I had major surgery the same day. And convalesced together. We healed beautifully and quickly and I firmly believe we did so well because we did it together. We kept Monet for more than two months, and missed him terribly when we had to pass him along to a permanent home. It was also during this period when Ivan came back to visit, so we had two invalids and a very crowded home. It was delightful!

❦ ❦ ❦

Penny (Foster #9) • We called her Penny Lane and sang the Beatle's song of the same name to her. She was an older female who had been a winner and so was treated well by her trainer. Penny was a brindle the color of an oxidized copper penny with eyes to match and very smart and self-possessed. So diplomatic was our Penny Lane that she managed to avoid any animosity even though we already had two dominant females—Brynna and Ragnell.

Penny had an accident in our care and we had to rush her to the all night emergency vet. She had bonded to us so fast, that when we had to leave her overnight she leaned toward us and looked completely betrayed. I can still feel her eyes boring into me. She knew how to do guilt very well.

❦ ❦ ❦

Robin (Foster #10) • Honey blonde with a black muzzle, Robin is an unusually tiny, perfectly formed female so very, very shy, she crowded into the far corner of her crate where she had to be kept separate from the other rescues that day. My daughter had to crawl in after her and lift her out. However, once she gained confidence with us, she was a delight. Sweet, obedient, affectionate, quiet. We fell in love with her even though she was slower to housebreak than any of the other dogs. She is cat safe, but curious. She barked when alarmed, but yodeled when she was happy, a particularly endearing trait when she joyfully met us at the door with her "song."

Sam (Foster #11) • Immediately renamed Samson by my husband due to his large size, Sam is a solid black male with no bald spots at all and a coat which felt softer and silkier than the finest panne velvet. He was so quiet, and well behaved that it was like not having an extra dog around at all. Sam is a non-dominant male who didn't "mark" anything and never made "mistakes" in the house.

Sam ignored our cat even when she jumped right over him on her way to stealing his food so it worked out very well that he went to a home with several cats. The inspection and adoption were done in our home which is a method we prefer as we like to meet the adopting family. It helps us so much with the parting since we become very attached to every dog in our care.

Ragnell The Ragster • I have another dog, a Cocker Spaniel named Ragnell (aka Rags, Ragster, Raggers and Rag Doll). She is so hyperactive, that in four years, I have only achieved two decent sketches of her. She gets along well with Mungo and Brynna and also with most of the fosters. However, she is an outdoors dog as

she becomes nervous inside. She also likes to bark at birds, planes, and all overhead traffic. We like to think of her as our own private Early Warning Defense System, keeping our airspace safe for democracy.

Epilogue • Topaz, our beloved cat, passed away in January. Mungo is still watching all her usual haunts for signs of her. He is a very sensitive dog, instinctively knowing when to lean against me and provide a moment of support. Ragnell has begun her move to being an "inside" dog. We fixed a new bed in the studio under the worktable which she just loves. She can then enter or leave the house by, what used to be, the cat door. This way, she is in charge of how much solitude she cares to enjoy.

We will soon add an additional dog door into the yard so she can continue to guard the airspace over our home and yard by barking and chasing birds, planes and kites. Inside, the ceiling fans in the house do cause her concern.

We have a new foster named Updike from "U" group. A tall male, blonde with black muzzle, he is playful and pretty with a huge appetite. An active family will be a great home for him. And as always, when he leaves we'll have moments of sadness but always have our memories of the dogs who we loved, and who loved us. . . .

Judith A. Brody

A Few Words in Homage to Our Four-Legged-Friends

Every dog has his day. *Miguel de Cervantes*

If you pick up a starving dog and make him prosperous, he will not bite you. This is the principal difference between a dog and a man.
Mark Twain

A dog teaches a boy fidelity, perseverance, and to turn around three times before lying down. *Robert Benchley*

Dogs are great assets to candidates, and the feeling seems to be engendered that if a dog loves the candidate, he can't be all bad.
Oliver Wendell Holmes

The great pleasure of a dog is that you may make a fool of yourself with him and not only will he not scold you, but he will make a fool of himself too.
Samuel Butler

Ever considered what they must think of us? I mean, here we come back from the grocery store with the most amazing haul—chicken, pork, half a cow... They must think we're the greatest hunters on earth.
Anne Tyler

What I can never forget is the feel of Old Joe's throat pressed against my upturned wrist as he swallowed and lapped and swallowed for what must have been almost a month? His moving throat seemed to hold secrets and a soul, and for that short while, I was almost Dog.
Clyde Edgeton

The greatest love is a mother's, then a dog's, then a sweetheart's.
Polish Proverb

No matter how little money and how few possessions you own, having a pet makes you rich. *Louis Saben*

Whoever said you can't buy happiness forgot about puppies. *Gene Hill*

I wonder what goes through his mind when he sees us peeing in his water bowl. *Penny Ward Moses*

The thing about a dog is, you can come home at any hour, in any condition, and the dog cares not. He, or she, is just glad to see you. *Lewis Grizzard*

Money will buy you a pretty good dog, but it won't buy you the wag of his tail. *Unknown*

Dogs are our link to paradise. They don't know evil or jealousy or discontent. To sit with a dog on a hillside on a glorious afternoon is to be back in Eden, where doing nothing was not boring, it was peace. *Milan Kundera*

Outside of a dog, a book is probably man's best friend. Inside of a dog, it's too dark to read. *Groucho Marx*

Until one has loved an animal, a part of one's self remains unawakened. *Anatole France*

Ever occur to you why some of us can be this much concerned with animal suffering? Because gov't is not. Why not? Animals don't vote. *Paul Harvey*

Happy would it be for thousands of people if they could stand at last before the Judgment Seat and say, I have loved as truly and I have lived as decently as my dog. . . .

Henry Ward Beecher

I think dogs are the most amazing creatures; they give unconditional love. For me they are the role model for being alive.

Gilda Radner

If you have men who will exclude any of God's creatures from the shelter of compassion and pity, you will deal likewise with their fellow men. *St. Francis of Assisi*

Qui me amat, amet et canem meum. (Love me, love my dog.)

St. Bernard

Do you think dogs will be in heaven? I tell you, they will be there long before any of us. *Robert Louis Stevenson*

All in town were still asleep, when the sun came up with a shout and leap. In the lonely street unseen by man, a little dog danced. And the day began. . . . *Rupert Brooke*

Fabulous Facts About Our Greyhound Friends

Ovid wrote of Greyhounds in his Metamorphoses.

The Greyhound is the second fastest animal on earth. For short distances it can run forty-five miles per hour, and only the cheetah, at seventy-five miles per hour, is faster.

Greyhounds hunt mostly by sight and, thus, must be fast in order to keep their prey in view.

More than five thousand years ago the ancient Egyptians used Greyhounds to hunt. They are one of the oldest breeds of dog. Queen Cleopatra and King Tutankhamen both had Greyhounds.

Greyhounds are the only canine mentioned in the Bible. (Proverbs 30:29-31)

A law passed during the reign of King Canute enforced a law in which the killing of a Greyhound was considered the equal of the killing of a man.

President Abraham Lincoln (United States) had a Greyhound on his coat-of-arms.

Fabulous Facts About Our Canine Friends

Dogs can detect various tastes such as sweet, sour, salty and bitter tastes but have less than one sixth the taste buds of humans.

A dog's ability to see is attuned more to movement than color. In keeping with their predator heritage, very slight movements will be noticeable to a dog even as humans would fail to notice the movement.

A dog's whiskers and the pads on their feet are particularly sensitive.

Dogs need less than one second to locate a sound and determine whether it needs more attention. This ability is heightened by the dogs ability to move their ears, or even one ear by itself.

A dog's sense of smell is extraordinary. Whereas a human has around five million odor receptors, a dog has over two hundred and twenty million. It is said that the wet nose of the dog helps capture scents.

Dogs, who may never know where their next meal is coming from, can swallow enormous chunks of food. This food is then digested in the stomach by concentrated stomach acids.

A dog's wide rib cage holds powerful lungs and a heart which can immediately pump the blood in the dog's circulatory system to its muscles. This allows the dog to run at speeds reached by only a few animals on earth.

The dog's heavily muscled neck allows for it to turn its head in almost a full radius—more than two hundred degrees.

The powerful bodies and legs of dogs are one of the great mechanical feats in the animal world. Dogs can run long distances which would exhaust many other animals.

Dogs use their toes as they walk, rather than the soles of their feet. Thus, they "grab" the earth as they run giving them an added powerful forward movement.

The dog family, Canidae, order Carnivora, contains about thirty-five species, grouped into fourteen genera, distributed throughout the world.

In the Northern Hemisphere, dog days are the hottest part of the summer. The term originated in ancient times. Sirius, the dog star, rose simultaneously with the sun, adding to the heat. This was said to create spells of madness in dogs.

೧   ೧   ೧